tempt

tempt

an anthology

ISBN: 978-1-60962-120-9

Tempt: An Anthology is dedicated to those who have loved, those who have lost, and those who have never been given the chance.

tempt
an anthology

Table of Contents

Preface

It is impossible to understand the connection between two people without confronting the beauty and significance of the physical and emotional intimacy between them. The authors within this anthology have written pieces focusing on and depicting lust, incandescent happiness, unrequited love, homophobia and secret love, and death.

Intimacy is one of the few things that can connect two individuals driven by the complete desire of love. The essence of physical touch and affection radiates through the words and ideologies of each work, epitomized in Oscar Wilde's letter to Lord Alfred Douglas. These works exemplify the great beauty of each lover's body and the overwhelming waves of emotion that encompass them. Lust provokes, shapes, and solidifies each piece.

Moreover, an underlying incandescent happiness is nextly presented in the pieces captured under Vita Sackville-West's letter to Virginia Woolf. As Sackville-West simply stated, "I am reduced to a thing that wants Virginia." That is merely what all the authors bluntly wanted: only and always their loved ones. The true and unconditionally pure act of love emanates through the voice of each piece.

Nothing does compare to the mournful but nevertheless vigorous emotion of love that is not returned. This unrequited love permeates through the works within this section, starting with Charlotte Brontë's letter to her professor, Constantin Héger, a teacher she knew would undoubtedly never love her back. Each author yearns for a love that is not there. The presence of this unreturned desire agonizes the bleeding hearts of their admirers. This heartrending lack of emotion is incredibly prominent throughout the life of each author. Each piece is pierced with infatuation, passion, and sorrowful longing.

This sorrow is once more depicted in Emily Dickinson's letter to her sister-in-law, Susan, fully illuminating the peril within the element of secret love. This hidden love, whether it be due to homophobia or frightful concealment, caustically sculpted the thoughts and influences of each secret lover within the section.

The anthology consummates with Virginia Woolf's suicide letter left to her husband Leonard. As the unbearable weight of the world fell upon her and the authors of this section, they submerged into desperation. Nevertheless, what each author fiercely felt for the ones they loved was pure and undeniable. While some may have been overcome by the fallacies of the world, they left with heavy hearts. As Woolf lastly stated, "I don't think two people could have been happier than we have been."

My Own Boy,

   Your sonnet is quite lovely, and it is a marvel that those red rose-leaf lips of yours should be made no less for the madness of music and song than for the madness of kissing. Your slim gilt soul walks between passion and poetry. I know Hyacinthus, whom Apollo loved so madly, was you in Greek days.

   Why are you alone in London, and when do you go to Salisbury? Do go there to cool your hands in the grey twilight of Gothic things, and come here whenever you like. It is a lovely place and lacks only you; but go to Salisbury first.

Always, with undying love, yours,

[11]

"Return, Gongyla"

Sappho

A deed
your lovely face

if not, winter
and no pain

I bid you,
Abanthis,
take up the lyre
and sing of
Gongyla as again desire
floats around you

the beautiful.
When you saw her dress
it excited you. I'm
happy.
The Kypros-born
once
blamed me

for praying
this word:
I want

The Well of Loneliness

Radclyffe Hall

But in such relationships as Mary's and Stephen's, Nature must pay for experimenting; she may even have to pay very dearly—it largely depends on the sexual mixture. A drop too little of the male in the lover, and mighty indeed will be the wastage. And yet there are cases— and Stephen's was one—in which the male will emerge triumphant; in which passion combined with real devotion will become a spur rather than a deterrent; in which love and endeavour will fight side by side in a desperate struggle to find some solution.

Thus it was that when Stephen returned from Morton, Mary divined, as it were by instinct, that the time of dreaming was over and past; and she clung very dose, kissing many times—

'Do you love me as much as before you went? Do you love me?' The woman's eternal question.

And Stephen, who, if possible, loved her more, answered almost brusquely: 'Of course I love you.'

Chapter 43, Part 1

"Memoirs"

John Addington Symonds

I used to take essays and verses at intervals
to Vaughan in the study which the scene
of his clandestine pleasures. It was a fairly
sized square room, dark, on the ground
floor, looking upon the street. On those
occasions my young brains underwent an
indescribable fermentation. I remember
once that, while we sat together reading
Greek iambics, he began softly to stroke
my right leg from knee to the thigh. This
insignificant caress, of which I should have
thought nothing two months earlier, and
which probably meant nothing, seemed
then disagreeably suggestive...

"Goblin Market"

Christina Rossetti

She cried, "Laura," up the garden,
"Did you miss me?
Come and kiss me.
Never mind my bruises,
Hug me, kiss me, suck my juices
Squeez'd from goblin fruits for you,
Goblin pulp and goblin dew.
Eat me, drink me, love me;
Laura, make much of me;
For your sake I have braved the glen
And had to do with goblin merchant men."

"A Woman Waits for Me"

Walt Whitman

A woman waits for me, she contains all,
nothing is lacking,
Yet all were lacking if sex were lacking, or if
the moisture of
   the right man were lacking.

Sex contains all, bodies, souls,
Meanings, proofs, purities, delicacies, re-
sults, promulgations,
Songs, commands, health, pride, the mater-
nal mystery, the
   seminal milk,
All hopes, benefactions, bestowals, all the
passions, loves,
   beauties, delights of the earth,
All the governments, judges, gods, follow'd
persons of the
   earth,
These are contain'd in sex as parts of itself
and justifications
   of itself.

Without shame the man I like knows and
avows the
   deliciousness of his sex,
Without shame the woman I like knows and

avows hers.

Now I will dismiss myself from impassive
women,
I will go stay with her who waits for me, and
with those
  women that are warm-blooded sufficient
for me,
I see that they understand me and do not
deny me,
I see that they are worthy of me, I will be
the robust
  husband of those women.

They are not one jot less than I am,
They are tann'd in the face by shining suns
and blowing
  winds,
Their flesh has the old divine suppleness
and strength,
They know how to swim, row, ride, wrestle,
shoot, run,
  strike, retreat, advance, resist, defend
themselves,
They are ultimate in their own right--they
are calm, clear,
  well-possess'd of themselves.

I draw you close to me, you women,
I cannot let you go, I would do you good,
I am for you, and you are for me, not only

for our own
  sake, but for others' sakes,
Envelop'd in you sleep greater heroes and
bards,
They refuse to awake at the touch of any
man but me.

It is I, you women, I make my way,
I am stern, acrid, large, undissuadable, but
I love you,
I do not hurt you any more than is neces-
sary for you,
I pour the stuff to start sons and daughters
fit for these
  States, I press with slow rude muscle,
I brace myself effectually, I listen to no
entreaties,
I dare not withdraw till I deposit what has
so long
  accumulated within me.

Through you I drain the pent-up rivers of
myself,
In you I wrap a thousand onward years,
On you I graft the grafts of the best-be-
loved of me and
  America,
The drops I distil upon you shall grow
fierce and athletic
  girls, new artists, musicians, and singers,
The babes I beget upon you are to beget

babes in their turn,
I shall demand perfect men and women
out of my love-
  spendings,
I shall expect them to interpenetrate with
others, as I and
  you interpenetrate now,
I shall count on the fruits of the gushing
showers of them, as
  I count on the fruits of the gushing
showers I give now,
I shall look for loving crops from the birth,
life, death,
  immortality, I plant so lovingly now.

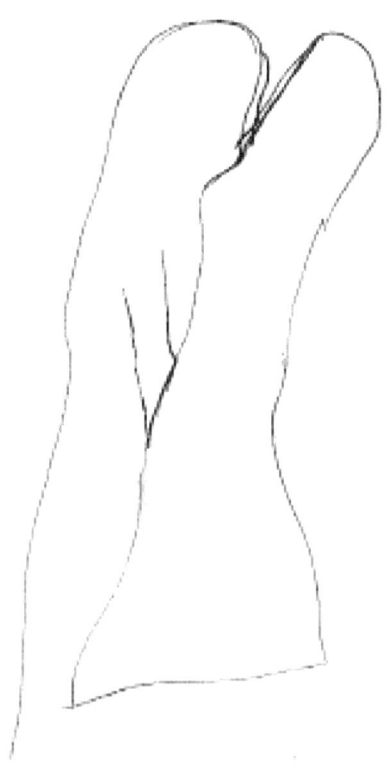

"Sonnet 17"

Richard Barnfield

Cherry-lipt Adonis in his snowie shape,
   Might not compare with his pure ivorie
white,
   On whose faire front a poet's pen may
write,
Whose roseate red excels the crimson grape,
His love-enticing delicate soft limbs,
   Are rarely fram'd t'intrap poore gazine
eies:
   His cheeks, the lillie and carnation dies,
With lovely tincture which Apollo's dims.
His lips ripe strawberries in nectar wet,
   His mouth a Hive, his tongue a ho-
ny-combe,
   Where Muses (like bees) make their man-
sion.
His teeth pure pearle in blushing correll set.
   Oh how can such a body sinne-procuring,
   Be slow to love, and quicke to hate, en-
during?

"Let me not to the marriage of true minds"

William Shakespeare

Let me not to the marriage of true minds
Admit impediments. Love is not love
Which alters when it alteration finds,
Or bends with the remover to remove:
O no! it is an ever-fixed mark,
That looks on tempests and is never shaken;
It is the star to every wand'ring bark,
Whose worth's unknown, although his
height be taken.
Love's not Time's fool, though rosy lips and
cheeks
Within his bending sickle's compass come;
Love alters not with his brief hours and
weeks,
But bears it out even to the edge of doom.
  If this be error and upon me prov'd,
  I never writ, nor no man ever lov'd.

"Silkworm"

Michelangelo

Kind to the world, but to itself unkind,
   A worm is born, that dying noiselessly
   Despoils itself to clothe fair limbs, and be
   In its true worth by death alone divined.
Oh, would that I might die, for her to find
   Raiment in my outworn mortality!
   That, changing like the snake, I might be
free
   To cast the slough wherein I dwell con-
fined!
Nay, were it mine, that shaggy fleece that
stays,
   Woven and wrought into a vestment fair,
   Around her beauteous bosom in such
bliss!
All through the day she'd clasp me! Would
I were
   The shoes that bear her burden! When
the ways
   Were wet with rain, her feet I then should
kiss!

"I Sing the Body Electric"

Walt Whitman

1

I sing the body electric;
The armies of those I love engirth me, and
I engirth them;
They will not let me off till I go with them,
respond to them,
And discorrupt them, and charge them full
with the charge of the soul.

Was it doubted that those who corrupt their
own bodies conceal themselves;
And if those who defile the living are as bad
as they who defile the dead?
And if the body does not do as much as the
soul?
And if the body were not the soul, what is
the soul?

2

The love of the body of man or woman
balks account, the body itself balks account,
That of the male is perfect, and that of the
female is perfect.

The expression of the face balks account;

But the expression of a well-made man
appears not only in his face;
It is in his limbs and joints also, it is curious-
ly in the joints of his hips and wrists;
It is in his walk, the carriage of his neck, the
flex of his waist and knees—dress does not
hide him;
The strong, sweet, supple quality he
has, strikes through the cotton and flan-
nel;
To see him pass conveys as much as the best
poem, perhaps more;
You linger to see his back, and the back of
his neck and shoulder-side.

The sprawl and fulness of babes, the bo-
soms and heads of women, the folds of their
dress, their style as we pass in the street, the
contour of their shape downwards,
The swimmer naked in the swimming-bath,
seen as he swims through the transparent
green-shine, or lies with his face up, and
rolls silently to and fro in the heave of the
water,
The bending forward and backward of
rowers in row-boats—the horseman in his
saddle,
Girls, mothers, house-keepers, in all their
performances,
The group of laborers seated at noon-time
with their open dinner-kettles, and their

wives waiting,
The female soothing a child—the farmer's
daughter in the garden or cow-yard,
The young fellow hoeing corn—the
sleigh-driver guiding his six horses through
the crowd,
The wrestle of wrestlers, two appren-
tice-boys, quite grown, lusty, good-natured,
native-born, out on the vacant lot at sun-
down, after work,
The coats and caps thrown down, the embrace of love and resistance,
The upper-hold and the under-hold,
the hair rumpled over and blinding the
eyes;
The march of firemen in their own cos-
tumes, the play of masculine muscle
through clean-setting trowsers and waist-
straps,
The slow return from the fire, the pause
when the bell strikes suddenly again, and
the listening on the alert,
The natural, perfect, varied attitudes—the
bent head, the curv'd neck, and the count-
ing;
Such-like I love—I loosen myself, pass freely, am at the mother's breast with the little
child,
Swim with the swimmers, wrestle with wrestlers, march in line with the firemen, and
pause, listen, and count.

3

I know a man, a common farmer—the
father of five sons;
And in them were the fathers of sons—and
in them were the fathers of sons.

This man was of wonderful vigor, calmness,
beauty of person;
The shape of his head, the pale yellow and
white of his hair and beard, and the im-
measurable meaning of his black eyes—the
richness and breadth of his manners,
These I used to go and visit him to see—he
was wise also;
He was six feet tall, he was over eighty years
old—his sons were massive, clean, bearded,
tan-faced, handsome;
They and his daughters loved him—all who
saw him loved him;
They did not love him by allowance—they
loved him with personal love;
He drank water only—the blood show'd like
scarlet through the clear-brown skin of his
face;
He was a frequent gunner and fisher—he
sail'd his boat himself—he had a fine one
presented to him by a ship-joiner—he had
fowling-pieces, presented to him by men
that loved him;
When he went with his five sons and many
grand-sons to hunt or fish, you would pick

him out as the most beautiful and vigorous of the gang.

You would wish long and long to be with him—you would wish to sit by him in the boat, that you and he might touch each other.

4
I have perceiv'd that to be with those I like is enough,
To stop in company with the rest at evening is enough,
To be surrounded by beautiful, curious, breathing, laughing flesh is enough,
To pass among them, or touch any one, or rest my arm ever so lightly round his or her neck for a moment—what is this, then?
I do not ask any more delight—I swim in it, as in a sea.

There is something in staying close to men and women, and looking on them, and in the contact and odor of them, that pleases the soul well;
All things please the soul—but these please the soul well.

5
This is the female form;

A divine nimbus exhales from it from head
to foot;
It attracts with fierce undeniable attrac-
tion!
I am drawn by its breath as if I were no
more than a helpless vapor—all falls aside
but myself and it;
Books, art, religion, time, the visible and
solid earth, the atmosphere and the clouds,
and what was expected of heaven or fear'd
of hell, are now consumed;
Mad filaments, ungovernable shoots play
out of it—the response likewise ungovernable;
Hair, bosom, hips, bend of legs, negligent
falling hands, all diffused—mine too diffused;
Ebb stung by the flow, and flow stung by
the ebb—love-flesh swelling and deliciously
aching;
Limitless limpid jets of love hot and enor-
mous, quivering jelly of love, white-blow
and delirious juice;
Bridegroom night of love, working surely
and softly into the prostrate dawn;
Undulating into the willing and yielding
day,
Lost in the cleave of the clasping and sweet-
flesh'd day.
This is the nucleus—after the child is
born of woman, the man is born of wom-

an;
This is the bath of birth—this is the
merge of small and large, and the outlet
again.

Be not ashamed, women—your privilege
encloses the rest, and is the exit of the
rest;
You are the gates of the body, and you are
the gates of the soul.

The female contains all qualities, and tem-
pers them—she is in her place, and moves
with perfect balance;
She is all things duly veil'd—she is both
passive and active;
She is to conceive daughters as well as sons,
and sons as well as daughters.

As I see my soul reflected in nature;
As I see through a mist, one with inexpress-
ible completeness and beauty,
See the bent head, and arms folded over the
breast—the female I see.

6
The male is not less the soul, nor more—he
too is in his place;
He too is all qualities—he is action and
power;
The flush of the known universe is in

him;
Scorn becomes him well, and appetite and
defiance become him well;
The wildest largest passions, bliss that is
utmost, sorrow that is utmost, become him
well—pride is for him;
The full-spread pride of man is calming and
excellent to the soul;
Knowledge becomes him—he likes it
always—he brings everything to the test of
himself;
Whatever the survey, whatever the sea and
the sail, he strikes soundings at last only
here;
(Where else does he strike soundings, except
here?)

The man's body is sacred, and the woman's
body is sacred;
No matter who it is, it is sacred;
Is it a slave? Is it one of the dull-faced immi-
grants just landed on the wharf?
Each belongs here or anywhere, just as
much as the well-off—just as much as
you;
Each has his or her place in the procession.

(All is a procession;
The universe is a procession, with measured
and beautiful motion.)

Do you know so much yourself, that you call
the slave or the dull-face ignorant?
Do you suppose you have a right to a
good sight, and he or she has no right to a
sight?
Do you think matter has cohered together
from its diffuse float—and the soil is on the
surface, and water runs, and vegetation
sprouts,
For you only, and not for him and
her?

7
A man's Body at auction;
I help the auctioneer—the sloven does not
half know his business.

Gentlemen, look on this wonder!
Whatever the bids of the bidders, they cannot be high enough for it;
For it the globe lay preparing quintillions of
years, without one animal or plant;
For it the revolving cycles truly and steadily
roll'd.

In this head the all-baffling brain;
In it and below it, the makings of heroes.

Examine these limbs, red, black, or
white—they are so cunning in tendon and

nerve;
They shall be stript, that you may see
them.

Exquisite senses, life-lit eyes, pluck, voli-
tion,
Flakes of breast-muscle, pliant back-bone
and neck, flesh not flabby, good-sized arms
and legs,
And wonders within there yet.

Within there runs blood,
The same old blood!
The same red-running blood!
There swells and jets a heart—there all pas-
sions, desires, reachings, aspirations;
Do you think they are not there because
they are not express'd in parlors and lec-
ture-rooms?

This is not only one man—this is the father of those who shall be fathers in their
turns;
In him the start of populous states and rich
republics;
Of him countless immortal lives, with
countless embodiments and enjoy-
ments.

How do you know who shall come from the
offspring of his offspring through the centu-

ries?
Who might you find you have come from
yourself, if you could trace back through the
centuries?

8
A woman's Body at auction!
She too is not only herself—she is the teem-
ing mother of mothers;
She is the bearer of them that shall grow
and be mates to the mothers.

Have you ever loved the Body of a woman?
Have you ever loved the Body of a
man?
Your father—where is your father?
Your mother—is she living? have you been
much with her? and has she been much
with you?
—Do you not see that these are exactly the
same to all, in all nations and times, all over
the earth?

If any thing is sacred, the human body is
sacred,
And the glory and sweet of a man, is the
token of manhood untainted;
And in man or woman, a clean, strong,
firm-fibred body, is beautiful as the most
beautiful face.

Have you seen the fool that corrupted his own live body? or the fool that corrupted her own live body?
For they do not conceal themselves, and cannot conceal themselves.

9

O my Body! I dare not desert the likes of you in other men and women, nor the likes of the parts of you;
I believe the likes of you are to stand or fall with the likes of the Soul, (and that they are the Soul;)
I believe the likes of you shall stand or fall with my poems—and that they are po-
ems,
Man's, woman's, child's, youth's, wife's, husband's, mother's, father's, young man's, young woman's poems;
Head, neck, hair, ears, drop and tympan of the ears,
Eyes, eye-fringes, iris of the eye, eye-brows, and the waking or sleeping of the lids,
Mouth, tongue, lips, teeth, roof of the mouth, jaws, and the jaw-hinges,
Nose, nostrils of the nose, and the parti-tion,
Cheeks, temples, forehead, chin, throat, back of the neck, neck-slue,
Strong shoulders, manly beard, scapula,

hind-shoulders, and the ample side-round
of the chest.

Upper-arm, arm-pit, elbow-socket, low-
er-arm, arm-sinews, arm-bones,
Wrist and wrist-joints, hand, palm, knuckles,
thumb, fore-finger, finger-balls, finger-joints,
finger-nails,
Broad breast-front, curling hair of the
breast, breast-bone, breast-side,
Ribs, belly, back-bone, joints of the back-
bone,
Hips, hip-sockets, hip-strength, inward and
outward round, man-balls, man-root,
Strong set of thighs, well carrying the trunk
above,
Leg-fibres, knee, knee-pan, upper-leg, under
leg,
Ankles, instep, foot-ball, toes, toe-joints, the
heel;
All attitudes, all the shapeliness, all the belongings of my or your body, or of any one's
body, male or female,
The lung-sponges, the stomach-sac, the
bowels sweet and clean,
The brain in its folds inside the skull-
frame,
Sympathies, heart-valves, palate-valves,
sexuality, maternity,
Womanhood, and all that is a woman—and
the man that comes from woman,

The womb, the teats, nipples, breast-
milk, tears, laughter, weeping, love-looks,
love-perturbations and risings,
The voice, articulation, language, whisper-
ing, shouting aloud,
Food, drink, pulse, digestion, sweat, sleep,
walking, swimming,
Poise on the hips, leaping, reclining, em-
bracing, arm-curving and tightening,
The continual changes of the flex of the
mouth, and around the eyes,
The skin, the sun-burnt shade, freckles,
hair,
The curious sympathy one feels, when
feeling with the hand the naked meat of the
body,
The circling rivers, the breath, and breathing it in and out,
The beauty of the waist, and thence of
the hips, and thence downward toward the
knees,
The thin red jellies within you, or within
me—the bones, and the marrow in the
bones,
The exquisite realization of health;
O I say, these are not the parts and poems
of the Body only, but of the Soul,
O I say now these are the Soul!

"Symphony in Yellow"

Oscar Wilde

An omnibus across the bridge
Crawls like a yellow butterfly,
And, here and there, a passer-by
Shows like a little restless midge.

Big barges full of yellow hay
Are moored against the shadowy wharf,
And, like a yellow silken scarf,
The thick fog hangs along the quay.

The yellow leaves begin to fade
And flutter from the Temple elms,
And at my feet the pale green Thames
Lies like a rod of rippled jade.

"Towards Democracy"

Edward Carpenter

"O disrespectable Democracy! I love you.
No white
   Angelic spirit are you now, but a black
and horned Ethiopian—your
   great grinning lips and teeth and power-
ful brow
   And huge limbs please me well....
You fill me with vision, and when the night
comes
   I see the forests upon your flanks and
your horns among
   The stars. I climb upon you and fulfil my
desire."

"Antique"

Arthur Rimbaud

Graceful son of Pan! Around your forehead
crowned with small flowers and berries,
your eyes, precious spheres, are moving.
Spotted with brownish wine lees, your
cheeks grow hollow. Your fangs are gleam-
ing. Your chest is like a lyre, jingling sounds
circulate between your blond arms. Your
heart beats in that belly where the double
sex sleeps. Walk at night, gently moving that
thigh, that second thigh and that left leg.

The Well of Loneliness

Radclyffe Hall

The quarrel that ensued would start Barbara's cough, which in turn would start Jamie's nerves vibrating. Then compassion, together with unreasoning anger and a sudden uprush of sex-frustration, would make her feel wellnigh beside herself—since owing to Barbara's failing health, these two could be lovers now in name only. And this forced abstinence told on Jamie's work as well as her nerves, destroying her music, for those who maintain that the North is cold, might just as well tell us that hell is freezing. Yet she did her best, the poor uncouth creature, to subjugate the love of the flesh to the pure and more selfless love of the spirit—the flesh did not have it all its own way with Jamie.

Chapter 50, Part 1

"Angelo Fusato"

John Addington Symond

. . . Yes, he was here. Our four hands,
laughing, made
   Brief havoc of his belt, shirt, trousers,
shoes:
   Till, mother-naked, white as lilies, laid
There on the counterpane, he bade me use
   Even as I willed his body. But Love
forbade—
   Love cried, 'Less than Love's best thou
shalt refuse!' . . .

"Love's Lordship"

Michelangelo

Why should I seek to ease intense desire
With still more tears and windy words of
grief,
When heaven, or late or soon, sends no
relief
To souls whom love hath robed around
with fire.

Why need my aching heart to death aspire,
When all must die? Nay, death beyond
belief
Unto these eyes would be both sweet and
brief,
Since in my sum of woes all joys expire!

Therefore because I cannot shun the blow
I rather seek, say who must rule my breast,
Gliding between her gladness and her woe?
If only chains and bands can make me
blest,
No marvel if alone and bare I go
An armed Knight's captive and slave con-
fessed.

"Shall I compare thee to a summer's day?"

William Shakespeare

Shall I compare thee to a summer's day?
Thou art more lovely and more temperate.
Rough winds do shake the darling buds of
May,
And summer's lease hath all too short a
date.
Sometime too hot the eye of heaven shines,
And often is his gold complexion dimmed;
And every fair from fair sometime declines,
By chance, or nature's changing course,
untrimmed;
But thy eternal summer shall not fade,
Nor lose possession of that fair thou ow'st,
Nor shall death brag thou wand'rest in his
shade,
When in eternal lines to Time thou grow'st.
 So long as men can breathe, or eyes can
see,
 So long lives this, and this gives life to
thee.

"El Beso"

Angelina Weld Grimké

Twilight—and you
Quiet—the stars;
Snare of the shine of your teeth,
Your provocative laughter,
The gloom of your hair;
Lure of you, eye and lip;
Yearning, yearning,
Languor, surrender;
Your mouth,
And madness, madness,
Tremulous, breathless, flaming,
The space of a sigh;
Then awakening—remembrance,
Pain, regret—your sobbing;
And again, quiet—the stars,
Twilight—and you.

Darling,

...In one way this solitary
existence is particularly
revealing — in the way
I can twist and change
in my attitudes towards
people with absolutely no
stimulus at all except
such as springs from
within me. I'll awaken
some morning just loving
you frightfully much
in some quite new
way and I may
not have sufficiently
rubbed the sleep
from my eyes to

have even looked at your
picture. It gives me
a strange, almost uncanny
feeling of autonomy.
And it is true that
we have had this loveliness
"near" together for I never
feel you too far away to
whisper to, and your dear
hair is always just
slipping through my fingers...
when I do good work it is
always always for you...
and the thought of you
now makes me a little
unbearably happy.
margaret.

"To My Excellent Friend Lucasia, On Our Friendship"

Katherine Philips

I did not live until this time
   Crowned my felicity,
When I could say without a crime,
   I am not thine, but thee.

This carcass breathed, and walked, and slept,
   So that the world believed
There was a soul the motions kept;
   But they were all deceived.

For as a watch by art is wound
   To motion, such was mine:
But never had Orinda found
   A soul till she found thine;

Which now inspires, cures and supplies,
   And guides my darkened breast:
For thou art all that I can prize,
   My joy, my life, my rest.

No bridegroom's nor crown-conqueror's mirth
   To mine compared can be:
They have but pieces of the earth,

I've all the world in thee.

Then let our flames still light and shine,
    And no false fear control,
As innocent as our design,
    Immortal as our soul.

"Calamus"

Walt Whitman

In paths untrodden,
In the growth by margins of pond-waters,
Escaped from the life that exhibits itself,
From all the standards hitherto publish'd,
from the
   pleasures, profits, conformities,
Which too long I was offering to feed my
soul,
Clear to me now standards not yet publish'd, clear to me
   that my soul,
That the soul of the man I speak for rejoic-
es in comrades,
Here by myself away from the clank of the
world,
Tallying and talk'd to here by tongues aro-
matic,
No longer abash'd, (for in this secluded spot
I can respond as I would not dare else-
where,)
Strong upon me the life that does not ex-
hibit itself, yet
   contains all the rest,
Resolv'd to sing no songs to-day but those
of manly
   attachment,

Projecting them along that substantial life,
Bequeathing hence types of athletic love,
Afternoon this delicious Ninth-month in my forty-first
   year,
I proceed for all who are or have been young men,
To tell the secret my nights and days,
To celebrate the need of comrades.

"On What Is Best"

Sappho

Some celebrate the beauty
of knights, or infantry,
or billowing flotillas
at battle on the sea.
Warfare has its glory,
but I place far above
these military splendors
the one thing that you love.

For proof of this contention
examine history:
we all remember Helen,
who left her family,
her child, and royal husband,
to take a stranger's hand:
her beauty had no equal,
but bowed to love's command.

As love then is the power
that none can disobey,
so too my thoughts must follow
my darling far away:
the sparkle of her laughter
would give me greater joy
than all the bronze-clad heroes

"Meeting at Night"

Robert Browning

The gray sea and the long black land;
And the yellow half-moon large and low:
And the startled little waves that leap
In fiery ringlets from their sleep,
As I gain the cove with pushing prow,
And quench its speed i' the slushy sand.

Then a mile of warm sea-scented beach;
Three fields to cross till a farm appears;
A tap at the pane, the quick sharp scratch
And blue spurt of a lighted match,
And a voice less loud, through joys and
fears,
Than the two hearts beating each to each!

The Picture of Dorian Grey

Oscar Wilde

. . . I believe that if one man were to live out his life fully and completely, were to give form to every feeling, expression to every thought, reality to every dream—I believe that the world would gain such a fresh impulse of joy that we would forget all the maladies of mediaevalism, and return to the Hellenic ideal—to something finer, richer than the Hellenic ideal, it may be. But the bravest man amongst us is afraid of himself. The mutilation of the savage has its tragic survival in the self-denial that mars our lives. We are punished for our refusals. Every impulse that we strive to strangle broods in the mind and poisons us. The body sins once, and has done with its sin, for action is a mode of purification. Nothing remains then but the recollection of a pleasure, or the luxury of a regret. The only way to get rid of a temptation is to yield to it. Resist it, and your soul grows sick with longing for the things it has forbidden to itself, with desire for what its monstrous laws have made monstrous and unlawful . . .

Chapter 2

"Awed by her Splendor"

Sappho

Awed by her splendor
stars near the lovely
moon cover their own
bright faces
when she
is roundest and lights
earth with her silver

"At the Touch of You"

Witter Bynner

At the touch of you,
As if you were an archer with your swift
hand at the bow,
The arrows of delight shot through my
body.

You were spring,
And I the edge of a cliff,
And a shining waterfall rushed over me.

"A Decade"

Amy Lowell

When you came, you were like red wine
and honey,
And the taste of you burnt my mouth with
its sweetness.
Now you are like morning bread,
Smooth and pleasant.
I hardly taste you at all for I know your
savour,
But I am completely nourished.

"Pederasty"

Marcel Proust

To Daniel Halévy

If I had money from a boundless mint-
and sinew enough in hands, lips, loins, I'd
shun the vanity of politics and print, and
leave—tomorrow? No, tonight!—for lawns
luminous with artificial green (without the
rustic flaws of frost and vermin), where I'd
forever be sleeping with one warm child
or other: François? Firmin? . . .For what is
manly mockery to me? Let Sodom's apples burn, acre by acre, I'd savor still the
sweat of those sweet limbs! Beneath a solar
gold, a lunar nacre, I'd… languish (an ars
moriendi of my own), deaf to the knell of
dreary Decency!

"Annabel Lee"

Edgar Allan Poe

It was many and many a year ago,
　In a kingdom by the sea,
That a maiden there lived whom you may know
　By the name of Annabel Lee;
And this maiden she lived with no other thought
　Than to love and be loved by me.

I was a child and *she* was a child,
　In this kingdom by the sea,
But we loved with a love that was more than love—
　I and my Annabel Lee;
With a love that the winged seraphs of Heaven
　Coveted her and me.

And this was the reason that, long ago,
　In this kingdom by the sea,
A wind blew out of a cloud, chilling
　My beautiful Annabel Lee;
So that her highborn kinsmen came
　And bore her away from me,
To shut her up in a sepulchre
　In this kingdom by the sea.

The angels, not half so happy in Heaven,
    Went envying her and me—
Yes!—that was the reason (as all men know,
    In this kingdom by the sea)
That the wind came out of the cloud by
night,
    Chilling and killing my Annabel Lee.

But our love it was stronger by far than the
love
    Of those who were older than we—
    Of many far wiser than we—
And neither the angels in Heaven above,
    Nor the demons down under the sea,
Can ever dissever my soul from the soul
    Of the beautiful Annabel Lee:

For the moon never beams, without bring-
ing me dreams
    Of the beautiful Annabel Lee;
And the stars never rise, but I feel the bright
eyes
    Of the beautiful Annabel Lee;
And so, all the night-tide, I lie down by the
side
    Of my darling—my darling—my life and
my bride,
    In her sepulchre there by the sea,
    In her tomb by the sounding sea.

"In the Forest"

Oscar Wilde

Out of the mid-wood's twilight
Into the meadow's dawn,
Ivory limbed and brown-eyed,
Flashes my Faun!

He skips through the copses singing,
And his shadow dances along,
And I know not which I should follow,
Shadow or song!

O Hunter, snare me his shadow!
O Nightingale, catch me his strain!
Else moonstruck with music and madness
I track him in vain!

"Bright Star"

John Keats

Bright star! would I were steadfast as thou
art—
  Not in lone splendour hung aloft the
night,
And watching, with eternal lids apart,
  Like Nature's patient sleepless Eremite,
The moving waters at their priestlike task
  Of pure ablution round earth's human
shores,
Or gazing on the new soft fallen mask
  Of snow upon the mountains and the
moors—
No—yet still steadfast, still unchangeable,
  Pillow'd upon my fair love's ripening
breast,
To feel for ever its soft fall and swell,
  Awake for ever in a sweet unrest,
Still, still to hear her tender-taken breath,
And so live ever—or else swoon to death.

"Love Returned"

Bayard Taylor

He was a boy when first we met;
    His eyes were mixed of dew and fire,
And on his candid brow was set
    The sweetness of a chaste desire:
But in his veins the pulses beat
    Of passion, waiting for its wing,
As ardent veins of summer heat
    Throb through the innocence of spring.

As manhood came, his stature grew,
    And fiercer burned his restless eyes,
Until I trembled, as he drew
    From wedded hearts their young dis-
guise.
Like wind-fed flame his ardor rose,
    And brought, like flame, a stormy rain:
In tumult, sweeter than repose,
    He tossed the souls of joy and pain.

So many years of absence change!
    I knew him not when he returned:
His step was slow, his brow was strange,
    His quiet eye no longer burned.
When at my heart I heard his knock,
    No voice within his right confessed:
I could not venture to unlock

Its chambers to an alien guest.

Then, at the threshold, spent and worn
    With fruitless travel, down he lay:
And I beheld the gleams of morn
    On his reviving beauty play.
I knelt, and kissed his holy lips,
    I washed his feet with pious care;
And from my life the long eclipse
    Drew off; and left his sunshine there.

He burns no more with youthful fire;
    He melts no more in foolish tears;
Serene and sweet, his eyes inspire
    The steady faith of balanced years.
His folded wings no longer thrill,
    But in some peaceful flight of prayer:
He nestles in my heart so still,
    I scarcely feel his presence there.

O Love, that stern probation o'er,
    Thy calmer blessing is secure!
Thy beauteous feet shall stray no more,
    Thy peace and patience shall endure!
The lightest wind deflowers the rose,
    The rainbow with the sun departs,
But thou art centred in repose,
    And rooted in my heart of hearts!

"Before the Dawn"

Federico García Lorca

But like love
the archers
are blind

Upon the green night,
the piercing saetas
leave traces of warm
lily.

The keel of the moon
breaks through purple clouds
and their quivers
fill with dew.

Ay, but like love
the archers
are blind!

"One Girl"

Sappho

I

Like the sweet apple which reddens upon
the topmost bough,
Atop on the topmost twig,—which the
pluckers forgot,
    somehow,—
Forget it not, nay; but got it not, for none
could get it till now.

II

Like the wild hyacinth flower which on the
hills is found,
Which the passing feet of the shepherds for
ever tear and
    wound,
Until the purple blossom is trodden in the
ground.

"How Do I Love Thee?"

Elizabeth Barrett Browning

How do I love thee? Let me count the ways.
I love thee to the depth and breadth and
height
My soul can reach, when feeling out of
sight
For the ends of Being and ideal Grace.
I love thee to the level of every day's
Most quiet need, by sun and candlelight.
I love thee freely, as men strive for Right;
I love thee purely, as they turn from Praise.
I love with a passion put to use
In my old griefs, and with my childhood's
faith.
I love thee with a love I seemed to lose
With my lost saints,—I love thee with the
breath,
Smiles, tears, of all my life!—and, if God
choose,
I shall but love thee better after death.

Mrs. Dalloway

Virginia Woolf

. . . The strange thing, on looking back, was
the purity, the integrity, of her feeling for
Sally. It was not like one's feeling for a man.
It was completely disinterested, and besides,
it had a quality which could only exist between women, between women just grown
up. It was protective, on her side; sprang
from a sense of being in league together, a
presentiment of something that was bound
to part them (they spoke of marriage
always as a catastrophe), which led to this
chivalry, this protective feeling which was
much more on her side than Sally's. For
in those days she was completely reckless;
did the most idiotic things out of bravado;
bicycled round the parapet on the terrace;
smoked cigars. Absurd, she was—very
absurd. But the charm was overpowering,
to her at least, so that she could remember
standing in her bedroom at the top of the
house holding the hot-water can in her
hands and saying aloud, "She is beneath
this roof. . . . She is beneath this roof!"

No, the words meant absolutely nothing to
her now. She could not even get an echo of

her old emotion. But she could remember going cold with excitement, and doing her hair in a kind of ecstasy (now the old feeling began to come back to her, as she took out her hairpins, laid them on the dressing-table, began to do her hair), with the rooks flaunting up and down in the pink evening light, and dressing, and going downstairs, and feeling as she crossed the hall "if it were now to die 'twere now to be most happy." That was her feeling—Othello's feeling, and she felt it, she was convinced, as strongly as Shakespeare meant Othello to feel it, all because she was coming down to dinner in a white frock to meet Sally Seton! . . .

Part 1

XI. "On your midnight pallet lying"

A. E. Housman

On your midnight pallet lying,
  Listen, and undo the door:
Lads that waste the light in sighing
  In the dark should sigh no more;
Night should ease a lover's sorrow;
Therefore, since I go to-morrow,
  Pity me before.

In the land to which I travel,
  The far dwelling, let me say—
Once, if here the couch is gravel,
  In a kinder bed I lay,
And the breast the darnel smothers
Rested once upon another's
  When it was not clay.

July 1844

Monsieur, I am well away that it is not my turn to write to you... at present my sight is too weak for writing— if I wrote a lot I would become blind. This weakness of sight is a terrible privation for me — without it, do you know what I would do, Monsieur? I would write a book and I would dedicate it to my literature master— to the only master I have ever had to you Monsieur.

October 1844

I am afraid of bothering you, I would just like to ask whether you heard from me at the beginning of May and then in the month of August? For all those six months I have been expecting a letter from you, Monsieur— six months of waiting—That is a very long time indeed.

[70]

January 1845

Forgive me then Monsieur if I take
the step of writing to you again—
How can I bear my life unless I
make an effort to alleviate its
sufferings?

I know that you will lose patience
with me when you read this letter
you will say that I am over-excited—
that I have black thoughts etc.
So be it Monsieur—I do not seek
to justify myself, I submit to all
kinds of reproaches—all I know—
is that I cannot—that I will
not resign myself to the total
loss of my master's friendship—
I would rather undergo the greatest
bodily pains than have my heart
constantly lacerated by searing
regrets. If my master withdraws
his friendship from me entirely I
shall be absolutely without hope—
if he gives me a little friendship—
a very little—I shall be content—
happy, I would have a motive for
living—for working—

[71]

November 1845

To tell the truth I have made painful efforts to endure until now the privation of imposed on myself; you, Monsieur — you cannot conceive what that means...

I will tell you candidly that during this time of waiting I have tried to forget you, for the memory of a person one believes one is never to see again, and whom one nevertheless greatly respects, torments the mind exceedingly and when one has suffered this kind of anxiety for one or two years, one is ready to do anything to regain peace of mind.

"A Red, Red Rose"

Robert Burns

O my Luve is like a red, red rose
   That's newly sprung in June;
O my Luve is like the melody
   That's sweetly played in tune.

So fair art thou, my bonnie lass,
   So deep in luve am I;
And I will luve thee still, my dear,
   Till a' the seas gang dry.

Till a' the seas gang dry, my dear,
   And the rocks melt wi' the sun;
I will love thee still, my dear,
   While the sands o' life shall run.

And fare thee weel, my only luve!
   And fare thee weel awhile!
And I will come again, my luve,
   Though it were ten thousand mile.

"Her Voice"

Oscar Wilde

The wild bee reels from bough to bough
  With his furry coat and his gauzy wing,
Now in a lily-cup, and now
  Setting a jacinth bell a-swing,
    In his wandering;
Sit closer love: it was here I trow
    I made that vow,

Swore that two lives should be like one
  As long as the sea-gull loved the sea,
As long as the sunflower sought the sun,—
  It shall be, I said, for eternity
    'Twixt you and me!
Dear friend, those times are over and done;
    Love's web is spun.

Look upward where the poplar trees
  Sway and sway in the summer air,
Here in the valley never a breeze
  Scatters the thistledown, but there
    Great winds blow fair
From the mighty murmuring mystical seas,
    And the wave-lashed leas.

Look upward where the white gull screams,
  What does it see that we do not see?

Is that a star? or the lamp that gleams
    On some outward voyaging argosy,—
        Ah! can it be
We have lived our livces in a land of
dreams!
        How sad it seems.

Sweet, there is nothing left to say
    But this, that love is never lost,
Keen winter stabs the breasts of May
    Whose crimson roses burst his frost,
        Ships tempest-tossed
Will find a harbour in some bay,
        And so we may.

And there is nothing left to do
    But to kiss once again, and part,
Nay, there is nothing we should rue,
    I have my beauty,—you your Art,
        Nay, do not start,
One world was not enough for two
        Like me and you.

"One Sea-Side Grave"

Christina Rosetti

Unmindful of the roses,
Unmindful of the thorn,
A reaper tired reposes
Among his gathered corn:
So might I, till the morn!

Cold as the cold Decembers,
Past as the days that set,
While only one remembers
And all the rest forget,—
But one remembers yet.

"THE DREAM OF FAME: October 1861"

Lewis Carroll

1.

He saw her once, and in the glance,
A moment's glance of meeting eyes,
His heart stood still in sudden trance,
He trembled with a sweet surprise-
As one that caught through opening skies
A distant gleam of Paradise.

2.

That summer eve his heart was light,
With lighter step he trod the ground,
And life was fairer in his sight,
And music was in every sound.
He blessed the world where there could be
So beautiful a thing as she.

3.

But days went by—he found her not;
And years rolled on—she never came;
Though ever round the fatal spot
A mocking whisper of her name
In hollow whispers seemed to roll
Through the dark chambers of his soul.

4.
From land to land he sought her face;
To him were neither night nor day;
The phantom he was doomed to chase
Still glided from his touch away;
And life that once had been so bright
Seemed but a dream of yesternight.

"He would not stay for me, and who can wonder"

A. E. Housman

He would not stay for me, and who can
wonder?
  He would not stay for me to stand and
gaze.
I shook his hand, and tore my heart in
sunder,
  And went with half my life about my ways.

"In Memoriam"

Alfred Lord Tennyson

XXVII.

I envy not in any moods
    The captive void of noble rage,
    The linnet born within the cage,
That never knew the summer woods:

I envy not the beast that takes
    His license in the field of time,
    Unfetter'd by the sense of crime,
To whom a conscience never wakes;

Nor, what may count itself as blest,
    The heart that never plighted troth
    But stagnates in the weeds of sloth;
Nor any want-begotten rest.

I hold it true, whate'er befall;
    I feel it, when I sorrow most;
    'Tis better to have loved and lost
Than never to have loved at all.

"Love's Philosophy"

Percy Bysshe Shelley

The fountains mingle with the river
And the rivers with the ocean,
The winds of heaven mix for ever
With a sweet emotion;
Nothing in the world is single,
All things by a law divine
In one another's being mingle—
Why not I with thine?

See the mountains kiss high heaven,
And the waves clasp one another;
No sister-flower would be forgiven
If it disdain'd its brother;
And the sunlight clasps the earth,
And the moonbeams kiss the sea—
What is all this sweet work worth
If thou kiss not me?

Untitled

Herman Melville

A man of a deep and noble nature had
seized me in this seclusion. . . . The soft rav-
ishments of the man spun me round about
in a web of dreams. . . . But already I feel
that Hawthorne had dropped germinous
seeds into my soul. He expands and deep-
ens down, the more I contemplate him;
and further and further shoots his strong
New-England roots into the hot soil in my
Southern soul.

The Well of Loneliness

Radclyffe Hall

. . . And so blinded was she by those gleams
of glory which the stars fling into the eyes
of young lovers, that she saw perfection
where none existed . . .

Chapter 19, Part 1

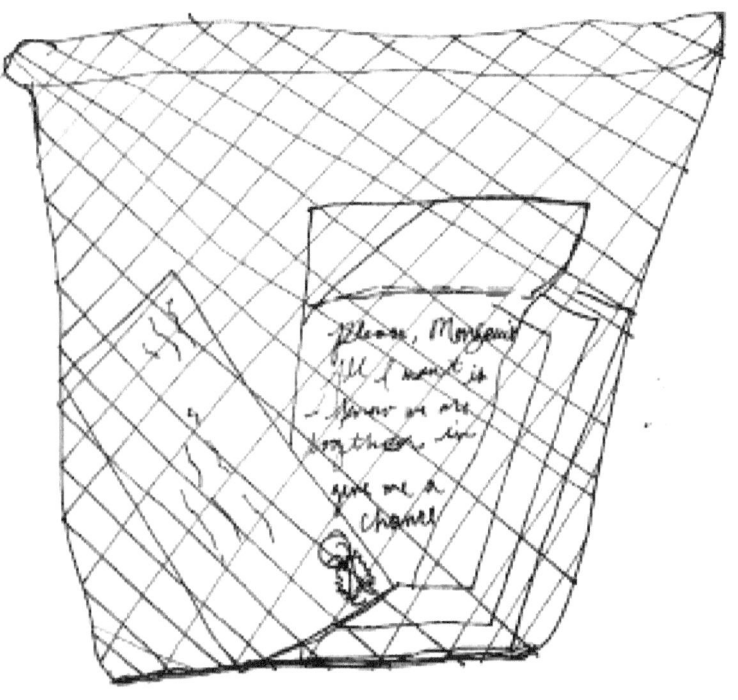

"Music When Soft Voices Die"

Percy Bysshe Shelley

Music, when soft voices die,
Vibrates in the memory—
Odours, when sweet violets sicken,
Live within the sense they quicken.

Rose leaves, when the rose is dead,
Are heaped for the beloved's bed;
And so thy thoughts, when thou art gone,
Love itself shall slumber on.

"Love is my sin and they dear virtue hate"

William Shakespeare

Love is my sin and thy dear virtue hate,
Hate of my sin, grounded on sinful loving:
O, but with mine compare thou thine own
state,
And thou shalt find it merits not reproving;
Or, if it do, not from those lips of thine,
That have profaned their scarlet ornaments
And seal'd false bonds of love as oft as mine,
Robb'd others' beds' revenues of their rents.
Be it lawful I love thee, as thou lovest those
Whom thine eyes woo as mine importune
thee:
Root pity in thy heart, that when it grows
Thy pity may deserve to pitied be.
   If thou dost seek to have what thou dost
hide,
   By self-example mayst thou be denied!

XVII. "Oh, when I was in love with you"

A. E. Housman

Oh, when I was in love with you
  Then I was clean and brave,
And miles around the wonder grew
  How well did I behave.

And now the fancy passes by
  And nothing will remain,
And miles around they'll say that I
  Am quite myself again.

I have but one thought, Susie,
this afternoon of June, and that of you.
and I have one prayer, only; Dear Susie,
that is for you. That you and I in hand as
we e'en do in heart, might ramble away
as children, among the woods and fields,
and forget these many years, and these
~~sorrowing~~ cares, and each become a child
again — I would it were so, Susie, and
when I look around me and find
myself alone, I sigh for you again;
little sigh, and vain sigh, which will
not bring you home . . .

I shall grow more and
more impatient until that
dear day comes, for till now
I have only mourned for you,
now I begin to hope for you.

"Towards Democracy"

Edward Carpenter

. . . The budding pens of love scorch all
over me - my skin
is too tight, I am ready to burst through
it—a flaming girdle
is round my middle. Eyes, hair, lips, hands,
waist, thighs—
O naked mad tremors; in the dark feeling
pasturing flames! . . .

"Two Loves"

Lord Alfred Douglas

'Sweet youth,
Tell me why, sad and sighing, thou dost
rove
These pleasant realms? I pray thee speak
me sooth
What is thy name?' He said, 'My name is
Love.'
Then straight the first did turn himself to
me
And cried, 'He lieth, for his name is Shame,
But I am Love, and I was wont to be
Alone in this fair garden, till he came
Unasked by night; I am true Love, I fill
The hearts of boy and girl with mutual
flame.'
Then sighing, said the other, 'Have thy will,
I am the love that dare not speak its name.'

"At a Dinner Party"

Amy Levy

With fruit and flowers the board is decked,
    The wine and laughter flow;
I'll not complain—could one expect
    So dull a world to know?

You look across the fruit and flowers,
    My glance your glances find.—
It is our secret, only ours,
    Since all the world is blind.

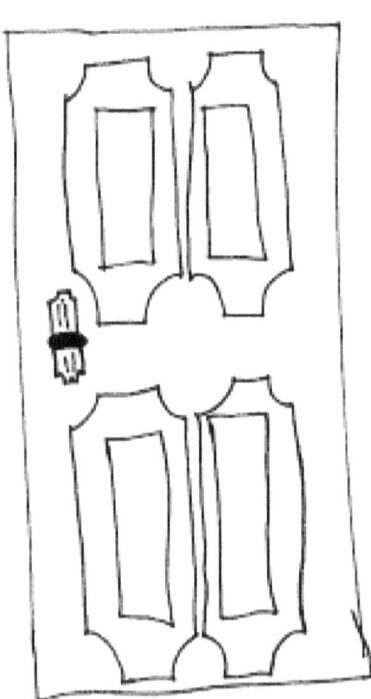

"Untitled"

M. R. Rodenbaugh

my hair is a jet black harbinger

white-blonde strands dipped in an oil spill
slick with fresh intention

she used to drink it in like champagne
pouring me out until the bubbles over-
flowed

now these tresses weep ebony
reflecting raven's feather blue
twin sister to the blood pooled in the cradle
of my orbital rim

a fist is a fruitful deterrent to
loving incorrect chromosomes

my pulse worships freely with the certainty
she'll never look at me again

after all,
she's into blondes

The Great Gatsby

F. Scott Fitzgerald

. . . It was nine o'clock—almost immediately afterward I looked at my watch and found it was ten. Mr. McKee was asleep on a chair with his sts clenched in his lap, like a photograph of a man of action. Taking out my handkerchief I wiped from his cheek the remains of the spot of dried lather that had worried me all the afternoon.

The little dog was sitting on the table looking with blind eyes through the smoke and from time to time groaning faintly. People disappeared, reappeared, made plans to go somewhere, and then lost each other, searched for each other, found each other a few feet away. Some time toward midnight Tom Buchanan and Mrs. Wilson stood face to face discussing in impassioned voices whether Mrs. Wilson had any right to mention Daisy's name.

'Daisy! Daisy! Daisy!' shouted Mrs. Wilson. 'I'll say it whenever I want to! Daisy! Dai——'

Making a short deft movement Tom Buchanan broke her nose with his open hand.

Then there were bloody towels upon the bathroom floor, and women's voices scolding, and high over the confusion a long broken wail of pain. Mr. McKee awoke from his doze and started in a daze toward the door. When he had gone half way he turned around and stared at the scene—his wife and Catherine scolding and consoling as they stumbled here and there among the crowded furniture with articles of aid, and the despairing figure on the couch bleeding fluently and trying to spread a copy of 'Town Tattle' over the tapestry scenes of Versailles. Then Mr. McKee turned and continued on out the door. Taking my hat from the chan- delier I followed.

'Come to lunch some day,' he suggested, as we groaned down in the elevator.

'Where?'

'A n y w h e r e .'

'Keep your hands off the lever,' snapped the elevator boy.

'I beg your pardon,' said Mr. McKee with dignity, 'I didn't know I was touching it.'

'All right,' I agreed, 'I'll be glad to.'

... I was standing beside his bed and he was sitting up between the sheets, clad in his underwear, with a great portfolio in his hands.

'Beauty and the Beast ... Loneliness ... Old Grocery Horse ... Brook'n Bridge ....'

Then I was lying half asleep in the cold lower level of the Pennsylvania Station, staring at the morning 'Tribune' and waiting for the four o'clock train. . .

"Untitled"

Emily Dickinson

To be Susan is Imagination,
To have been Susan, a Dream—
What depths of Domingo in that torrid
Spirit!

"The Affectionate Shepherd"

Richard Barnfield

Scarce had the morning starre hid from the
light
    Heavens crimson canopie with stars
bespangled,
    But I began to rue th' unhappy sight
    Of that faire boy that had my hart
intangled;
    Cursing the time, the place, the sense,
the sin;
    I came, I saw, I viewd, I slipped in.

    If it be sinne to love a sweet-fac'd boy,
    Whose amber locks trust up in golden
tramels
    Dangle adowne his lovely cheekes with
joy,
    When pearle and flowers his faire haire
enamels;
    If it be sinne to love a lovely lad,
    Oh then sinne I, for whom my soule is
sad.

    His ivory-white and alablaster skin
    Is staind throughout with rare vermil-
lion red,
    Whose twinckling starrie lights doe never

blin

    To shine on lovely Venus, Beauties bed;
    But as the lillie and the blushing rose,
    So white and red on him in order growes.

    Upon a time the nymphs bestird them-
selves
    To trie who could his beautie soonest
win;
    But he accounted them but all as elves,
    Except it were the faire Queene Guen-
dolen:
    Her he embrac'd, of her was beloved,
    With plaints he proved, and with teares
he moved.

    But her an old man had beene sutor too,
     That in his age began to doate againe;
    Her would he often pray, and often woo,
     When through old age enfeebled was his
braine:
    But she before had lov'd a lustie youth,
    That now was dead, the cause of all her
ruth.

    And thus it hapned, Death and Cupid
met
    Upon a time at swilling Bacchus house,
    Where daintie cates upon the boord were
set,
    And goblets full of wine to drinke

carouse:
    Where Love and Death did love the licor
so,
    That out they fall and to the fray they
goe.

    And having both their quivers at their
backe
      Fild full of arrows; th' one of fatall
steele,
    The other all of gold; Deaths shaft was
black,
      But Loves was yellow: Fortune turnd her
wheele,
      And from Deaths quiver fell a fatall shaft,
      That under Cupid by the winde was waft.

    And at the same time by ill hap there fell
      Another arrow out of Cupids quiver,
    The which was carried by the winde at
will,
      And under Death the amorous shaft did
shiver:
    They being parted, Love tooke up Deaths
dart,
    And Death tooke up Loves arrow for his
part.

    Thus as they wandred both about the
world,
      At last Death met with one of feeble

age:

    Wherewith he drew a shaft and at him hurld

      The unknowne arrow with a furious rage,

    Thinking to strike him dead with Deaths blacke dart;

    But he, alas, with Love did wound his hart!

    This was the doting foole, this was the man

      That lov'd faire Guendolena, Queene of Beautie;

    Shee cannot shake him off, doo what she can,

      For he hath vowd to her his soules last duety:

    Making him trim upon the holydaies,

    And crownes his love with garlands made of baies.

    Now doth he stroke his beard, and now againe

      He wipes the drivel from his filthy chin;

    Now offers he a kisse, but high Disdaine

      Will not permit her hart to pity him:

    Her hart more hard than adamant or steele,

    Her hart more changeable than Fortunes wheele.

But leave we him in love up to the eares,
    And tell how Love behav'd himselfe
abroad;
    Who seeing one that mourned still in
teares,
    A young man groaning under Loves
great load,
    Thinking to ease his burden, rid his
paines,
    For men have griefe as long as life re-
maines.

    Alas, the while that unawares he drue
    The fatall shaft that Death had dropt
before,
    By which deceit great harme did then
insue,
    Stayning his face with blood and filthy
goare:
    His face, that was to Guendolen more
deere
    Than love of lords, or any lordly peere.

    This was that faire and beautifull young
man,
    Whom Guendolena so lamented for;
    This is that Love whom she doth curse
and ban,
    Because she doth that dismall chaunce
abhor:
    And if it were not for his mothers sake,

Even Ganimede himselfe she would
forsake.

Oh would shee would forsake my Ganimede,
    Whose sugred love is full of sweete
delight,
    Upon whose forehead you may plainely
reade
    Loves pleasure grav'd in yvorie tables
bright:
    In whose faire eye-balls you may clearely
see
    Base Love still staind with foule indignitie.

Oh would to God he would but pitty
mee,
    That love him more than any mortall
wight!
    Then he and I with love would soone
agree,
    That now cannot abide his sutors sight.
    O would to God, so I might have my fee,
    My lips were honey, and thy mouth a bee!

Then shouldst thou sucke my sweete and
my faire flower,
    That now is ripe and full of honey-ber-
ries;
    Then would I leade thee to my pleasant
bower,

Fild full of grapes, of mulberries, and
cherries:
   Then shouldst thou be my waspe or else
my bee,
   I would thy hive, and thou my honey, bee.

I would put amber bracelets on thy
wrests,
   Crownets of pearle about thy naked
armes:
   And when thou sitst at swilling Bacchus
feasts
   My lips with charmes should save thee
from all harmes:
   And when in sleepe thou tookst thy chief-
est pleasure,
   Mine eyes should gaze upon thine eyelids
treasure.
   And every morne by dawning of the day,
   When Phoebus riseth with a blushing
face,
   Silvanus chappel-clarkes shall chaunt a
lay,
   And play thee hunts-up in thy resting
place:
   My coote thy chamber, my bosome thy
bed
   Shall be appointed for thy sleepy head.

And when it pleaseth thee to walke
abroad,

Abroad into the fields to take fresh ayre,
  The meades with Floras treasure should
be strowde,
  The mantled meaddowes, and the fields
so fayre.
  And by a silver well with golden sands
  Ile sit me downe, and wash thine yvory
hands.

  And in the sweltring heate of summer
time,
    I would make cabinets for thee, my love;
    Sweet-smelling arbours made of eglan-
tine
    Should be thy shrine, and I would be
thy dove.
    Cool cabinets of fresh greene laurell
boughs
    Should shadow us, ore-set with thicke-set
eughes.

  Or if thou list to bathe thy naked limbs
    Within the cristall of a pearle-bright
brooke,
    Paved with dainty pibbles to the brims,
    Or cleare, wherein thyselfe thyselfe
mayst looke;
    Weele goe to Ladon, whose still trickling
noyse
    Will lull thee fast asleepe amids thy joyes.

Or if thoult goe unto the river side,
  To angle for the sweet freshwater fish,
  Arm'd with thy implements that will
abide,
  Thy rod, hooke, line, to take a dainty
dish;
  Thy rods shall be of cane, thy lines of
silke,
  Thy hooks of silver, and thy bayts of
milke.

  Or if thou lov'st to hear sweet melodie,
  Or pipe a round upon an oaten reede,
  Or make thyselfe glad with some myrth-
full glee,
  Or play them musicke whilst thy flocke
doth feede.
  To Pans owne pype Ile helpe my lovely
lad,
  Pans golden pype, which he of Syrinx
had.

  Or if thou darst to climbe the highest
trees
  For apples, cherries, medlars, peares, or
plumbs,
  Nuts, walnuts, filbeards, chestnuts, cervi-
ces,
  The hoary peach, when snowy winter
comes;
  I have fine orchards full of mellowed

frute,
    Which I will give thee to obtaine my sute.

    Not proud Alcynous himselfe can vaunt
      Of goodlier orchards or of braver trees
    Than I have planted; yet thou wilt not
graunt
      My simple sute, but like the honey bees
    Thou suckst the flowre till all the sweet be
gone,
    And loost mee for my coyne till I have
none.

    Leave Guendolen, sweet hart; though she
be faire,
      Yet is she light; not light in vertue shin-
ing,
    But light in her behaviour, to impaire
      Her honour in her chastities declining;
    Trust not her teares, for they can wanton-
nize,
    When teares in pearle are trickling from
her eyes.
    If thou wilt come and dwell with me at
home,
      My sheepcote shall be strowed with new
greene rushes:
    Weele haunt the trembling prickets as
they rome
      About the fields, along the hauthorne
bushes;

I have a pie-bald curre to hunt the hare,
So we will live with daintie forrest fare.

Nay, more than this, I have a garden plot,
   Wherein there wants nor hearbs, nor
roots, nor flowers;
   Flowers to smell, roots to eate, hearbs for
the pot,
   And dainty shelters when the welkin
lowers:
   Sweet-smelling beds of lillies, and of
roses,
   Which rosemary banks and lavender
incloses.

There growes the gilliflowre, the mynt,
the dayzie
   Both red and white, the blue-veynd
violet;
   The purple hyacinth, the spyke to please
thee,
   The scarlet dyde carnation bleeding yet:
   The sage, the savery, and sweet mar-
gerum,
   Isop, tyme, and eye-bright, good for the
blinde and dumbe.

   The pinke, the primrose, cowslip and
daffodilly,
   The hare-bell blue, the crimson cullum-
bine,

Sage, lettis, parsley, and the milke-white
lilly,
    The rose and speckled flowre cald sops-
in-wine,
    Fine pretie king-cups, and the yellow
bootes,
    That growes by rivers and by shallow
brookes.

    And manie thousand moe I cannot name
        Of hearbs and flowers that in gardens
grow,
    I have for thee, and coneyes that be tame,
        Young rabbets, white as swan, and
blacke as crow;
    Some speckled here and there with dain-
tie spots:
    And more I have two mylch and mil-
ke-white goates.

    All these and more Ile give thee for thy
love,
        If these and more may tyce thy love
away:
    I have a pidgeon-house, in it a dove,
        Which I love more than mortall tongue
can say.
    And last of all Ile give thee a little lambe
        To play withall, new weaned from her
dam.

But if thou wilt not pittie my complaint,
  My teares, nor vowes, nor oathes, made
to thy beautie:
  What shall I doo but languish, die, or
faint,
    Since thou dost scorne my teares, and
my soules duetie:
  And teares contemned, vowes and oaths
must faile,
  And where teares cannot, nothing can
prevaile.

  Compare the love of faire Queene Guen-
dolin
    With mine, and thou shalt [s]ee how she
doth love thee:
  I love thee for thy qualities divine,
    But shee doth love another swaine above
thee:
  I love thee for thy gifts, she for hir pleasure;
  I for thy vertue, she for beauties treasure.

  And alwaies, I am sure, it cannot last.
    But sometime Nature will denie those
dimples:
  Insteed of beautie, when thy blossom's
past,
    Thy face will be deformed full of
wrinckles;
  Then she that lov'd thee for thy beauties

sake,
   When age drawes on, thy love will soone
forsake.

   But that I lov'd thee for thy gifts divine,
      In the December of thy beauties wan-
ing,
   Will still admire with joy those lovely eine,
      That now behold me with their beauties
baning.
   Though Januarie will never come againe,
      Yet Aprill yeres will come in showers of
raine.

   When will my May come, that I may
embrace thee?
      When will the hower be of my soules
joying?
   Why dost thou seeke in mirth still to dis-
grace mee?
      Whose mirth's my health, whose griefe's
my harts annoying:
   Thy bane my bale, thy blisse my bless-
ednes,
   Thy ill my hell, thy weale my welfare is.

   Thus doo I honour thee that love thee so,
      And love thee so, that so doo honour
thee
   Much more than anie mortall man doth
know,

Or can discerne by love or jealozie:
But if that thou disdainst my loving ever,
Oh happie I, if I'had loved never!

FINIS.

Plus fellis quam mellis amor.

The Well of Loneliness

Radclyffe Hall

. . . Our love may be faithful even unto death and beyond–yet the world will call it unclean. We may harm no living creature by our love; we may grow more perfect in understanding and in charity because of our loving; but all this will not save you from the scourge of a world that will turn away its eyes from your noblest actions, finding only corruption and vileness in you. You will see men and women defiling each other, laying the burden of their sins upon their children. You will see unfaithfulness, lies and deceit among those whom the world views with approbation. You will find that many have grown hard of heart, have grown greedy, selfish, cruel and lustful; and then you will turn to me and will say: 'You and I are more worthy of respect than these people. Why does the world persecute us, Stephen?' And I shall answer: 'Because in this world there is only toleration for the so-called normal'. . .

Chapter 27, Part 3

"Lady of Shallott"

Alfred Lord Tennyson

Part I

On either side the river lie
Long fields of barley and of rye,
That clothe the wold and meet the sky;
And through the field the road runs by
    To many-towered Camelot;
And up and down the people go,
Gazing where the lilies blow
Round an island there below,
    The island of Shalott.

Willows whiten, aspens quiver,
Little breezes dusk and shiver
Through the wave that runs for ever
By the island in the river
    Flowing down to Camelot.
Four grey walls, and four grey towers,
Overlook a space of flowers,
And the silent isle imbowers
    The Lady of Shalott.

By the margin, willow-veiled,
Slide the heavy barges trailed
By slow horses; and unhailed
The shallop flitteth silken-sailed
    Skimming down to Camelot:

But who hath seen her wave her hand?
Or at the casement seen her stand?
Or is she known in all the land,
        The Lady of Shalott?

Only reapers, reaping early
In among the bearded barley,
Hear a song that echoes cheerly
From the river winding clearly,
        Down to towered Camelot:
And by the moon the reaper weary,
Piling sheaves in uplands airy,
Listening, whispers "'Tis the fairy
        Lady of Shalott."

"A woman's face with nature's own hand painted"

William Shakespeare

A woman's face with nature's own hand
painted,
Hast thou, the master mistress of my pas-
sion;
A woman's gentle heart, but not acquainted
With shifting change, as is false women's
fashion:
An eye more bright than theirs, less false in
rolling,
Gilding the object whereupon it gazeth;
A man in hue all hues in his controlling,
Which steals men's eyes and women's souls
amazeth.
And for a woman wert thou first created;
Till Nature, as she wrought thee, fell a-dot-
ing,
And by addition me of thee defeated,
By adding one thing to my purpose nothing.
    But since she prick'd thee out for wom-
en's pleasure,
    Mine be thy love and thy love's use their
treasure.

"Her breast is fit for pearls"

Emily Dickinson

Her breast is fit for pearls,
But I was not a "Diver"—
Her brow is fit for thrones
But I have not a crest.
Her heart is fit for home
I—a Sparrow—build there
Sweet of twigs and twine
My perennial nest.

"HANDS"

Sherwood Anderson

...Out of the dream Wing Biddlebaum made a picture for George Willard. In the picture men lived again in a kind of pastoral golden age. Across a green open country came clean-limbed young men, some afoot, some mounted upon horses. In crowds the young men came to gather about the feet of an old man who sat beneath a tree in a tiny garden and who talked to them.

Wing Biddlebaum became wholly inspired. For once he forgot the hands. Slowly they stole forth and lay upon George Willard's shoulders. Something new and bold came into the voice that talked. "You must try to forget all you have learned," said the old man. "You must begin to dream. From this time on you must shut your ears to the roaring of the voices."

Pausing in his speech, Wing Biddlebaum looked long and earnestly at George Willard. His eyes glowed. Again he raised the hands to caress the boy and then a look of horror swept over his face.

With a convulsive movement of his body, Wing Biddlebaum sprang to his feet and thrust his hands deep into his trousers pockets. Tears came to his eyes. "I must be getting along home. I can talk no more with you," he said nervously.

Without looking back, the old man had hurried down the hillside and across a meadow, leaving George Willard perplexed and frightened upon the grassy slope. With a shiver of dread the boy arose and went along the road toward town. "I'll not ask him about his hands," he thought, touched by the memory of the terror he had seen in the man's eyes. "There's something wrong, but I don't want to know what it is. His hands have something to do with his fear of me and of everyone…"

"My River Runs to Thee"

Emily Dickinson

My River runs to thee.
Blue sea, wilt thou welcome me?
My river awaits reply.
Oh! Sea, look graciously.

I'll fetch thee brooks
From spotted nooks.
Say, sea,
Take me!

"TWO OLD CHERRY TREES STILL IN BLOOM"

Saikaku Ihara

...Living there was this masterless samurai who in his youth had lost hope of ever regaining official status in a lord's service and now lived day to day selling his various personal belongings. His only companion day in and day out was an old man of about the same age, his partner in games of go. A spotted Pekinese was his only other companion. No one ever came by even for brief visits.

One day, his hemp kimono was soaked with sweat and he felt too listless even to stir up a breeze with his fan, so the old man hurried the arrival of evening with an early bath and began washing the sweat from his body. His old companion watched him and thought, "Ah, the ravages of time!" Affectionately, he massaged the man's bony spine. He was grieved by the wrinkles below the man's waist and soon sank into tearful sobs.

"Sing the Tune Loudly, Hide the Mirror Bright

Yesterday, Youth; Today, a Head of White

"Seeing how this body of yours has changed
reminded me of that poem. How sad to
think that not so long ago we sang songs
and played games together . . . ." They held
hands and lamented until the bath water
turned cold...

"Symposium"

Plato

...and when one of them meets the other
half, the actual half of himself, whether he
be a lover of youth or a lover of another
sort, the pair are lost in an amazement of
love and friendship and intimacy and one
will not be out of the other's sight, as I may
say, even for a moment...

"What Mystery Pervades a Well!"

Emily Dickinson

What mystery pervades a well!
That water lives so far—
A neighbor from another world
Residing in a jar

Whose limit none have ever seen,
But just his lid of glass—
Like looking every time you please
In an abyss's face!

The grass does not appear afraid,
I often wonder he
Can stand so close and look so bold
At what is awe to me.

Related somehow they may be,
The sedge stands next the sea—
Where he is floorless
And does no timidity betray

But nature is a stranger yet;
The ones that cite her most
Have never passed her haunted house,
Nor simplified her ghost.

To pity those that know her not

Is helped by the regret
That those who know her, know her less
The nearer her they get.

Dearest,
I feel certain I am
going mad again. I feel we
can't go through another
of those terrible times.
And I shan't recover
this time. I begin to hear
voices, and I can't concen-
trate. So I am doing
what seems the best thing
to do. You have given me

the greatest
possible happiness.
You have been in
every way all that

anyone could be. I don't think two people could have been happier till this terrible disease came. I can't fight any longer. I know that I am spoiling your life, that without me you could work. And you will I know. You see I can't even write this properly. I can't read. What I want to say is I owe all the happiness of my life to you. You have been entirely patient with

me and incredibly good.
I want to say that —
everybody knows it. If
anybody could have saved
me it would have been
you. Everything has gone
from me but the certaint
of your goodness. I can't
go on spoiling your life
any longer.

I don't think two
people could have been
happier than we have
been.

LVII. "Yiou smile upon your friend to-day"

A. E. Housman

You smile upon your friend to-day,
  To-day his ills are over;
You hearken to the lover's say,
  And happy is the lover.

'Tis late to hearken, late to smile,
  But better late than never;
I shall have lived a little while
  Before I die for ever.

"O Captain! My Captain!"

Walt Whitman

O Captain! my Captain! our fearful trip is
done, The ship has
weather'd every rack,
   the prize we sought is won, The port is
near, the bells I hear,
the people all exulting,
   While follow eyes the steady keel, the ves-
sel grim and daring;
But O heart! heart! heart!
   O the bleeding drops of red, Where on
the deck my Captain
lies, Fallen cold and dead.
   O Captain! my Captain! rise up and
hear the bells; Rise up—for you the flag is
flung—for
   you the bugle trills,

   For you bouquets and ribbon'd
wreaths—for you the shores
     a-crowding,
   For you they call, the swaying mass, their
eager faces
turning;
      Here Captain! dear father!
      This arm beneath your head!
      It is some dream that on the deck,

You've fallen cold and dead.
    My Captain does not answer, his lips are
pale and still,
    My father does not feel my arm, he has
no pulse nor will,
The ship is anchor'd safe and sound, its
voyage closed and
done,
    From fearful trip, the victor ship, comes
in with object won;
        Exult, O shores, and ring, O bells!
        But I with mournful tread,
            Walk the deck my c=Captain lies,
            Fallen cold and dead.

"Melancholy Surprise"

Marcel Proust

So tired of having suffered, more tired of
having loved.
Life, having charmed me with its open
spaces,
Now tightens around me its monotonous
glove,
And my dream, seeing the walls around it
rise,
Curls up in melancholy surprise.

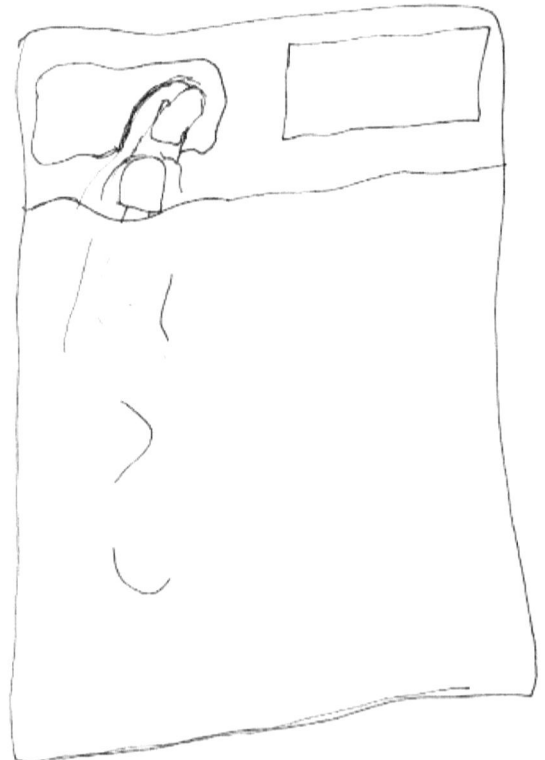

"THE PSYCHOGENESIS OF A CASE OF HOMOSEXUALITY IN A WOMAN"

Sigmund Freud

A beautiful and clever girl of eighteen, belonging to a family of good standing, had aroused displeasure and concern on the part of her parents by the tender passion with which she pursued a certain lady, about ten years older than herself. The parents asserted that this lady, in spite of her distinguished name, was no better than a cocotte. It was said to be a well-known fact that she lived with a married woman-friend, having intimate relations with her, while at the same time she carried on promiscuously with a number of men. The girl did not contradict these evil reports, but she continued to be none the less enamoured of the lady in question, although she herself was by no means lacking in a sense of decency and propriety. No prohibitions and no supervision hindered the girl from seizing every one of the rare opportunities of being together with her beloved friend, of ascertaining all her habits, of waiting for her for hours outside her door or at a tram halt, of sending her gifts of flowers, and so on. It was evident that this one interest had swallowed up all others. The girl did not concern herself with any further educational studies, placed no value on social functions or girlish pleasures, and kept up relations only with those friends who could help her in the matter or serve as confidantes. The parents could not say to what lengths their daughter had gone in her relations to the questionable lady, or whether the limits of devoted admiration had already been exceeded. They had never remarked in their daughter any interest in young men, nor any pleasure at their attentions, and, on the other hand, they were quite sure that her present attachment for a woman was only a continuation in a marked degree of the feeling she had displayed of recent years for other members of her own sex, which had already aroused her father's suspicion and severity...

XLIX. "Think no more, lad; laugh, be jolly"

A. E. Housman

Think no more, lad; laugh, be jolly:
  Why should men make haste to die?
Empty heads and tongues a-talking
Make the rough road easy walking,
And the feather pate of folly
  Bears the falling sky.

Oh, 'tis jesting, dancing, drinking
  Spins the heavy world around.
If young hearts were not so clever,
Oh, they would be young for ever:
Think no more; 'tis only thinking
  Lays lads underground.

"Henry V"

William Shakespeare

Upon these words I came and cheer'd him
up:
He smiled me in the face, raught me his
hand,
And, with a feeble gripe, says 'Dear my
lord,
Commend my service to me sovereign.'
So did he turn and over Suffolk's neck
He threw his wounded arm and kiss'd his
lips;
And so espoused to death, with blood he
seal'd
A testament of noble-ending love.
The pretty and sweet manner of it forced
Those waters from me which I would have
stopp'd;
But I had not so much of man in me,
And all my mother came into mine eyes
And gave me up to tears.

Act IV, Scene vi

"Maud"

Alfred Lord Tennyson

Queen rose of the rosebud garden of girls,
    Come hither, the dances are done,
In gloss of satin and glimmer of pearls,
    Queen lily and rose in one;
Shine out, little head, sunning over with
curls,
    To the flowers, and be their sun.

There has fallen a splendid tear
    From the passion-flower at the gate.
She is coming, my dove, my dear;
    She is coming, my life, my fate;
The red rose cries, "She is near, she is
near;"
    And the white rose weeps, "She is late;"
The larkspur listens, "I hear, I hear;"
    And the lily whispers, "I wait."

She is coming, my own, my sweet;
    Were it ever so airy a tread,
My heart would hear her and beat,
    Were it earth in an earthy bed;
My dust would hear her and beat,
    Had I lain for a century dead,
Would start and tremble under her feet,
    And blossom in purple and red.

"Paul's Case"

Willa Cather

. . . He rose and moved about with a painful effort, succumbing now and again to attacks of nausea. It was the old depression exaggerated; all the world had become Cordelia Street. Yet somehow he was not afraid of anything, was absolutely calm; perhaps because he had looked into the dark corner at last and knew. It was bad enough, what he saw there, but somehow not so bad as his long fear of it had been. He saw everything clearly now. He had a feeling that he had made the best of it, that he had lived the sort of life he was meant to live, and for half an hour he sat staring at the revolver. But he told himself that was not the way, so he went downstairs and took a cab to the ferry.

When Paul arrived in Newark he got off the train and took another cab, directing the driver to follow the Pennsylvania tracks out of the town. The snow lay heavy on the roadways and had drifted deep in the open fields. Only here and there the dead grass or dried weed stalks projected, singularly black, above it. Once well into the country,

Paul dismissed the carriage and walked, floundering along the tracks, his mind a medley of irrelevant things. He seemed to hold in his brain an actual picture of everything he had seen that morning. He remembered every feature of both his drivers, of the toothless old woman from whom he had bought the red flowers in his coat, the agent from whom he had got his ticket, and all of his fellow passengers on the ferry. His mind, unable to cope with vital matters near at hand, worked feverishly and deftly at sorting and grouping these images. They made for him a part of the ugliness of the world, of the ache in his head, and the bitter burning on his tongue. He stooped and put a handful of snow into his mouth as he walked, but that, too, seemed hot. When he reached a little hillside, where the tracks ran through a cut some twenty feet below him, he stopped and sat down.

The carnations in his coat were drooping with the cold, he noticed, their red glory all over. It occurred to him that all the flowers he had seen in the glass cases that first night must have gone the same way, long before this. It was only one splendid breath they had, in spite of their brave mockery at the winter outside the glass; and it was a losing game in the end, it seemed, this revolt against the homilies by which the world is run. Paul took one of the blossoms carefully from his coat and scooped a little hole in the snow, where he covered it up. Then he dozed awhile, from his weak condition, seemingly insensible to the cold.

The sound of an approaching train awoke him, and he started to his feet, remembering only his resolution, and afraid lest he should be too late. He stood watching the approaching locomotive, his teeth chattering, his lips drawn away from them in a frightened smile; once or twice he glanced nervously sidewise, as though he were being watched. When the right moment came, he jumped. As he fell, the folly of his haste occurred to him with merciless clearness, the vastness of what he had left undone. There flashed through his brain, clearer than ever before, the blue of Adriatic water, the yellow of Algerian sands.

He felt something strike his chest, and that his body was being thrown swiftly through the air, on and on, immeasurably far and fast, while his limbs were gently relaxed. Then, because the picture-making mechanism was crushed, the disturbing visions flashed into black, and Paul dropped back into the immense design of things . . .

"Remorse"

August von **Platen**

How I started up in the night, in the night,
　Drawn on without rest or reprieval!
The streets with their watchmen were lost
to my sight,
　　As I wandered so light
　In the night, in the night,
　Through the gate with the arch medie-
val.

The mill-brook rushed from its rocky
height;
　I leaned o'er the bridge in my yearning;
Deep under me watched I the waves in
their flight,
　　As they glided so light
　In the night, in the night,
　Yet backward not one was returning.

O'erhead were revolving, so countless and
bright,
　The stars in melodious existence;
And with them the moon, more serenely
bedight;—
　　They sparkled so light
　In the night, in the night,
　Through the magical, measureless dis-

tance.

And upward I gazed in the night, in the
night,
   And again on the waves in their fleeting;
Ah woe! thou hast wasted thy days in de-
light;
      Now silence thou, light
    In the night, in the night,
   The remorse in thy heart that is beating.

"The Ballad of Reading Gaol"

Oscar Wilde

He did not wear his scarlet coat,
  For blood and wine are red,
And blood and wine were on his hands
  When they found him with the dead,
The poor dead woman whom he loved,
  And murdered in her bed.

He walked amongst the Trial Men
  In a suit of shabby grey;
A cricket cap was on his head,
  And his step seemed light and gay;
But I never saw a man who looked
  So wistfully at the day.

I never saw a man who looked
  With such a wistful eye
Upon that little tent of blue
  Which prisoners call the sky,
And at every drifting cloud that went
  With sails of silver by.

IX. "On moonlit heath and lonesome bank"

A. E. Housman

On moonlit heath and lonesome bank
  The sheep beside me graze;
And yon the gallows used to clank
  Fast by the four cross ways.

A careless shepherd once would keep
  The flocks by moonlight there,*
And high amongst the glimmering sheep
  The dead man stood on air.

They hang us now in Shrewsbury jail:
  The whistles blow forlorn,
And trains all night groan on the rail
  To men that die at morn.

There sleeps in Shrewsbury jail to-night,
  Or wakes, as may betide,
A better lad, if things went right,
  Than most that sleep outside.

And naked to the hangman's noose
  The morning clocks will ring
A neck God made for other use
  Than strangling in a string.

And sharp the link of life will snap,
  And dead on air will stand
Heels that held up as straight a chap
  As treads upon the land.

So here I'll watch the night and wait
  To see the morning shine,
When he will hear the stroke of eight
  And not the stroke of nine;

And wish my friend as sound a sleep
  As lads' I did not know,
That shepherded the moonlit sheep
  A hundred years ago.

"In Memoriam"

Alfred Lord Tennyson

L.
Be near me when my light is low,
When the blood creeps, and the nerves
prick
And tingle; and the heart is sick,
And all the wheels of Being slow.

Be near me when the sensuous frame
Is rack'd with pangs that conquer trust;
And Time, a maniac scattering dust,
And Life, a fury slinging flame.

Be near me when my faith is dry,
And men the flies of latter spring,
That lay their eggs, and sting and sing
And weave their petty cells and die.

Be near me when I fade away,
To point the term of human strife,
And on the low dark verge of life
The twilight of eternal day.

Contributing authors

Oscar Wilde
Sappho
Radclyffe Hall
John Addington Symonds
Christina Rossetti
Walt Whitman
Richard Barnfield
William Shakespeare
Michelangelo
Edward Carpenter
Arthur Rimbaud
Angelina Weld Grimké
Margaret Mead
Katherine Philips
Robert Browning
Witter Bynner
Amy Lowell
Marcel Proust
Edgar Allen Poe
John Keats
Bayard Taylor

Federico García Lorca
Elizabeth Barrett Browning
Virginia Woolf
A.E. Housman
Charlotte Brontë
Robert Burns
Lewis Carroll
Alfred Lord Tennyson
Percy Bysshe Shelley
Herman Melville
Emily Dickinson
Lord Alfred Douglas
Amy Levy
M.R. Rodenbaugh
F. Scott Fitzgerald
Sherwood Anderson
Saikaku Ihara
Plato
Sigmund Freud
Willa Cather
August von Platen